Saint Edith Stein

Saint Edith Stein
(Saint Teresa Benedicta of the Cross, OCD)

Blessed by the Cross

Written by
Mary Lea Hill, FSP

Illustrated by
Mari Goering

Pauline
BOOKS & MEDIA
Boston

Library of Congress Cataloging-in-Publication Data

Hill, Mary Lea.

    Saint Edith Stein (Saint Teresa Benedicta of the Cross, O.C.D.) : blessed by the Cross / written by Mary Lea Hill ; illustrated by Mari Goering.

    p. cm. — (Encounter the saints series ; 5)

    Summary: A biography of the Jewish philosopher and convert to Catholicism who was put to death at Auschwitz during World War II and canonized by Pope John Paul II in 1998.

    ISBN 0-8198-7036-6 (pbk.)

    1. Stein, Edith, 1891–1942—Juvenile literature. 2. Christian saints—Germany—Biography—Juvenile literature. [1. Stein, Edith, 1891–1942. 2. Saints. 3. Women—Biography.] I. Goering, Mari, 1948– ill. II. Title. III. Series.

BX4700.S74 H55 1999
282'.092—dc21
[B]
                            99-058644

Printed and published in the U.S.A. by Pauline Books & Media, 50 Saint Pauls Avenue, Boston, MA 02130-3491.

www.pauline.org

Pauline Books & Media is the publishing house of the Daughters of St. Paul, an international congregation of women religious serving the Church with the communications media.

1 2 3 4 5 6   05 04 03 02 01 00

Encounter the Saints Series

Saint Anthony of Padua
Fire and Light

Saint Bernadette Soubirous
Light in the Grotto

Saint Edith Stein
Blessed by the Cross

Saint Elizabeth Ann Seton
Daughter of America

Saint Francis of Assisi
Gentle Revolutionary

For other children's titles on the Saints,
visit our Website: www.pauline.org

CONTENTS

1

THE BOXCAR

It was so dark. She could feel, hear and even smell the other people, but she could see no one. *There must not be any stars out tonight,* Sister Benedicta thought, straining to see even a sliver of light. *Dear God, it's 1942! Who would have thought that such a thing could happen now?*

They had been moving very steadily for a couple of hours. The constant click, clack, clack of the train's wheels pounding down the track filled the awful silence. Sister Benedicta was able to recollect her thoughts a bit and pray. *Thank you, Lord, for allowing me to be here with my people. Have mercy....*

All around the nun was a chorus of muffled sighs and moans. She suddenly became aware of soft sobbing right next to her. "Are you crying?"

"I can't get my mother to talk to me," a desperate little voice whimpered. "She only cries. She won't answer me."

"Your Mama is very tired, dear. Things

will get better, you'll see," Sister Benedicta soothed. "Tell me, what's your name?"

"Edith Weiss."

"Edith! My, that was my name, too. Now I'm called Sister Benedicta. Here, can you take this?" Sister Benedicta said, as she tried to place a handkerchief in little Edith's unseen hand. "Better now?" she asked. "Edith, you know that even when mamas are very, very tired, they are special people."

"Really?"

"Oh, yes! They are a special gift from God. God made mothers so that he could love us more."

"What about fathers?" asked the little girl.

"Certainly, fathers, too. God is our Father, isn't that so?" She touched the tired little face leaning against her arm. "Yes! The King of the universe is our Father, Edith. Even though we wish he would show it more clearly now, I'm certain he's caring for us right here in this train. Our fathers and mothers can't always give us what we want, or what they know would be best.... But even when they can't give us these things, they still love us very, very much." Sister Benedicta paused and gently stroked Edith's tear-stained cheek. "Do you believe this? Of course, you do. Right now our Heavenly Father would like to give us only what is good and comfortable and warm. But because he doesn't, do you think he loves us less?"

Little Edith nestled even further into the unseen folds of Sister Benedicta's robes. She let out a tiny muffled sigh.

"Not less, little Edith, but so much more! He is our Father—our loving Father. We are his chosen ones. Now no more talking for a while. Try to rest. I won't let you fall. Close your eyes. Think of God's love."

Sister Benedicta caressed the child's hair and soon felt the little girl relax, her head nodding. She knew the little one was dozing, even if fitfully. "Oh, Jesus," she whispered, "please protect these young ones... and all of us, who are your Father's children."

Half dozing herself now, Sister Benedicta felt her mother's arms around her, hearing her loving words. In her mind, it was that frightening day years ago in 1893 when her father had died. Mama Stein was gently rocking her youngest daughter. "Don't cry, my darling. Papa has gone to heaven, but he will continue to watch over his little girl. At this very moment, he is probably telling

God what a good girl his little Edith is. Two years old, but so good."

"Me, too, Mama? Me, too!" wailed four-year-old Erna. Mama reached out and pulled her close too.

It was always that way, Edith and Erna, Erna and Edith. They were the two youngest children in the Stein family. It seemed impossible to speak of one without the other. The two little girls were alike in many ways and yet so different in others. The older children called them "Open" and "Closed." Erna was a simple, direct child, "clear as water," while Edith was more complex and seemed to be a book "sealed with seven seals."

2

THE CROW & THE PUSSYCAT

From the window of her little office Mama Stein gazed at her two youngest daughters. They loved to play in the lumberyard. *I'm so fortunate*, Mama thought, *to be able to work so close to home and my children*. Her husband, Siegfried, had established the lumber business, which she herself now ran. No one had thought a widow with seven children would be able to keep such a business going, but Auguste Stein was an intelligent and resourceful woman who put great trust in God.

"Oh, Mama," Frieda, Frau Stein's second daughter, called from her desk. "Look at little Edith! She's just so smart."

"My Edith is a bit *too* smart sometimes," smiled Mama. "Look at her out there in the yard drilling Erna on her lessons. Why, she's hardly old enough for kindergarten! What are we to expect in the future?"

"Here they come for supper," Else, the oldest Stein daughter suddenly called from upstairs.

A door slammed and two little sets of legs came dashing up the stairs.

"My," twenty-four-year-old Paul exclaimed, swiveling in his chair, "you two are so fast. You're all swish and giggles. Maybe we should enter you in the national races." He stood and strained as if trying to follow a race at the track. "Can you see it now? 'Neck and neck miniature ponies cross the finish line in a blaze of glory, leaving everyone else behind in the dust!'"

"Oh, Paul, don't tease them so much," said Else as she grabbed one of the two and began to brush the sawdust from her dress.

"Yes, be careful, Paul," laughed Arno in typical teenage fashion. "Remember the Crow will squawk and peck you, and the Pussy will hiss and scratch you to death."

"I'm *not* a crow, Arno." Erna was insulted.

Darting over to where he sat, Edith glared at him. This only caused Arno to flap one imaginary wing. With the other hand, he reached down to pet Edith. "Here Pussy, Pussy!" he cooed.

"Stop being such a pest, Arno. I'm going to be angry with you," called Else. "We want a little peace for Mama when she comes in from the yard, don't we? She'll be tired."

At this the teasers and their little victims looked at each other and began giggling and laughing. Just then Mama walked in the door. At the sight of the merriment, she smiled lovingly from one to the other. "How pleased I am to be blessed with such good children. Noisy, yes, but nice."

"I can, too!" shouted the annoyed little girl.

"Prove it, Pussy," Paul pressed.

"OK, I will!" With that, Edith recited a ballad of the great German poet, Schiller. It was a perfect mimicry of the way she had heard Frieda practice it for school.

"Well, did you all hear that? What reward shall we give the kitten?" Paul asked as he lifted his little sister onto his shoulders.

With hands firmly planted on her hips, Edith announced very solemnly, "I don't need a reward, but I've decided what I want for my birthday."

Amused, the whole family turned to see what would come next.

"All I want for my birthday is school!"

"I'm going to be six years old and I want to go to the Viktoriaschule (Victoria School), just like Erna."

"But, dear," protested Mama, "the year is half over and you can't even read or write yet."

"I'll learn quickly, Mama. I learned all those poems, didn't I? Else will help me get in."

"Well, Mama, I think our little genius deserves a chance," responded Paul, bouncing Edith up and down on his shoulders.

"Just because I teach at the Viktoriaschule," protested Else, "you think I can obtain exceptions for my family?" Else glanced from Mama to Paul, from Rosa to Frieda, then from Arno to Erna. It was obvious that protests were useless. Under the beaming smile of the little victor she agreed. "OK, I'll try my best."

3

THE DROPOUT

Six-year-old Edith astonished everyone by quickly moving to the head of class that first year of school. That was to become her permanent position throughout her student years. Edith did not succeed without effort, but because she was a "go-getter," as she defined herself. It was at school that she felt most at home.

Perhaps because Edith was the youngest of the seven Stein children, she felt a need to prove her abilities. Sometimes her enthusiasm got the best of her. One teacher had to remind little Edith to patiently await her turn to be called on for answers. Several times she had skipped up the aisle toward the teacher waving her hand, "I know it! I know the answer! Just ask me!"

Her family and teachers always rewarded Edith's schoolwork with praise that embarrassed her. She preferred to work quietly, secure that she knew the correct answers and that she wrote intelligent reports.

"Turn, toward me, please! Really, Edith,

do you have to begin reading so early in the morning?" Rosa was trying to comb her younger sister's hair, but the child was so fascinated by her history book that she paid no attention to the plea.

Edith admitted that intense study helped her focus her ever-wandering mind. "I eat my books," she explained. Despite this concentration on study, Erna described Edith as an excellent companion, involved in every school activity and always ready to help her friends.

In her little kingdom of school and family, Edith's early years flew by in a swirl of happiness. She was a natural student. She was always at the top of her class, always enthused about knowledge. What a surprise it was to her family then when thirteen-year-old Edith announced one night that she would not be going back to school the following year. All eyes around the supper table stared at her in disbelief.

"You must be crazy, Edie!" Erna exclaimed. "You're the best student in the family, and you don't want to prepare for college?"

Noticing Edith's silence, Mama put a finger to her lips. "It seems Edith has made up her mind," she quietly observed. "Let's say no more for now. Let her be. She's worked very hard. A little break might be the best thing for her right now."

So Edith spent the next eight months in the city of Hamburg, helping her married sister Else with her three children. As Mama had hoped, the change worked wonders for her youngest daughter. When Edith returned home, Mama was pleased to see that her confused teenager was now a young woman.

Edith was growing up. The experience had changed her in many ways. She was no longer a thin little child. Her hair was no longer blond, but dark brown. Unfortunately, she had completely abandoned prayer. But Mama would be patient. Perhaps it would pass.

Now home in Breslau, Edith delighted in her new freedom. Not having to study or care for Else's children, she spent more time socializing with other young people. There was time now for rowing, tennis, hiking, and music. She had, in fact, in those months discovered a new talent. It was the ability to get whatever she wanted with a mere glance. Perhaps this new talent stemmed from her passion for drama. As she put it, Shakespeare had become "her daily bread."

It could also be due to the charm of her blossoming personality. She was a fascinating combination of shyness and boldness. And, although she didn't seem to notice it, Edith was a very attractive young woman. She was short and petite. Her large, dark brown eyes were soft and deep. She could be serious one minute and laughing contagiously the next.

"What now, Edith?" Mama ventured to ask.

"You know, Mama," Edith said thoughtfully, "I'm really not yet sure what I want to do."

"If you'd like a suggestion from me, I think you should go back to school, Edith. Else told me how good you were with the children. Perhaps you should prepare to be a teacher."

Suddenly, a light crept over Edith's face. She perked up. "Mama! I think you're right! I'll need a little tutoring to catch up to the others. Some math and some Latin should do it. Then I can take the examination and… and…."

Mama was beaming, too, content that Edith was home and happy again.

Edith eased right back into school. It was more enjoyable now. She was more relaxed. She still excelled in most subjects and found herself in much demand as a tutor to her companions. Because of her thoughtfulness, her popularity grew. She became the unofficial class spokesperson. On one occasion, she had suggested that the class go on a trip for a particular holiday, rather than prepare the usual school program. She was unanimously elected to present the proposal to the principal. Overcome with shyness, Edith put a popular finger puppet on her hand and proceeded to relate the request through this little character. The principal was won over. The outing was a great success. But the train ride home was a different story.

"OK, Edith. It's your turn. Remember, this is *Forfeit* we're playing. You have to wait in the next car."

"Hurry up!" she pleaded.

"We'll try, Edith. Now, go! Good-bye!"

Each of her classmates took a piece of paper and wrote down a "good" point and a "bad" point about Edith. Martha ran to the end doorway and called Edith back.

"Finished so soon?" she asked.

"Oh, you were easy."

Edith sat down in the middle of the group to await their judgment. It was difficult to listen to the list of praises. She squirmed nervously. *What would the negatives be?* she wondered.

"Walks too fast."

"Doesn't place her test sheets where it's easy to read them."

"Is altogether too smart and knows it."

"Gloats over the misfortunes of others."

Poor Edith couldn't believe her ears. *Gloats over the misfortunes of others?* This last one was too much. It just couldn't be true. Tears came quickly. Now she was even more embarrassed than before. She had never let anyone see her crying.

"How...how could anyone think that?" she sobbed. "It's...it's just terrible!" She was inconsolable for the rest of the trip. She kept searching through memories to find something she had said or done to give even one of her friends the idea that she took pleasure in thinking or talking about other people's problems. *I know kindness is more important than anything. It's more important than being right. When have I ever?... It's so unfair!*

Later the author of that comment apologized. The others had thought it would be a harmless joke. True to form, Edith accepted the apology, happy to renew the friendship. But the whole incident did cause her to be even more attentive to others in the future.

Sometime after, another companion made a "negative" comment: "You're much too critical of others, Edith." This time she realized that it *was* true. She *was* overly critical and she did actually think of herself as being perfect.

"I guess those of us who are very concerned about goodness automatically think of ourselves as being good already," she admitted sadly. "I'll have to try harder to be kind."

4

THE ADVENTURER

After graduation Edith spent four semesters at Breslau University. Then she approached her mother. "Mama, I'd like to go somewhere I've never been before."

A bit startled, Mama Stein could only ask, "Where would that be, dear?"

"Ooh! I know," Erna interrupted. "To our dream university at Heidelberg! You know, Mama, the two of us often planned to go there. It's such an old, romantic city."

"Now, Mama! Erna! Everyone! You know that I'm going to be a teacher. I've been studying psychology, but it doesn't satisfy me. I want to switch to phenomenology. I've read books about it. Now I want to study with the great master, Edmund Husserl, in Gottingen. It will be an adventure."

"What on earth is this fen...nom...meno ...nology?" blurted the ever-practical Rosa. "And why can't you study it right here in Breslau?"

"It's a new school of philosophical thought, Rosa. Unlike many modern philosophers,

Husserl and his students believe we can reach truth by studying reality around us. You know, the truth *in* the things that exist...."

"Oh, for heaven's sake, Edith. You don't need a new teacher to tell you that. Even we could do that!" Rosa was obviously exasperated as she stood there with her broom frozen in mid-air.

"I'm sure you could," Edith soothed. "Even though philosophy doesn't seem very practical, it is an important science. And you must admit there are plenty of false ideas around today. Edmund Husserl is the most original thinker alive. He wants to prepare people who can see through all the errors. *And* he teaches in Gottingen, so I have to go there."

"Well, dear, I'm content to know that God is truth. I don't need to go any further than that. And I don't like the idea of you leaving home again." This seemed to be Mama's last word on the subject. "However," she concluded, "you might be interested in reading this letter from your cousin Richard."

Edith scooped up the letter from the dining room table. Richard's wife, Nelli, had added a few words. It seemed that Richard had some friends who often joined the young couple, but there were few young ladies to balance out their social gatherings. "Could Erna or Edith come to Gottingen to study?" Nelli pleaded.

That settled things for Edith.

"You know what's best for your studies, dear," Mama suddenly announced. "After all, you are twenty-one."

Edith sank slowly into her chair. "Thank you, Mama," she smiled. A new adventure was about to begin....

5

PHILOSOPHY

Edith enthusiastically settled into student life in Gottingen. This was a whole new world for her. She immersed herself in the classes, seminars, and student activities. Edith was encouraged by the acceptance she found among the other students of Husserl. Even that great "master" himself had been impressed to find that this young girl had read his book before coming to Gottingen. "Not the small one," he had recounted to friends, "but the gigantic one. And she had a good grasp of what I was trying to say in it!"

Her companions were kind and the city was charming. However, Edith soon discovered that philosophy required more discipline and energy than she had ever put into study before. The other students were so far advanced that she had to struggle to keep up. She missed her family and friends, too. "I think I'm getting discouraged," she admitted one day.

Was there anything other than philosophy to which Edith could have applied her brilliance? Was it really impractical, as some people suggested? Besides, wasn't philosophy a man's world? Would she be able to find a teaching position after graduation?

Suddenly all of her personal problems were overshadowed by the outbreak of World War I in July of 1914. One by one her friends were leaving the university to join the military. Under these circumstances, Edith felt that she couldn't remain in her ivory tower of learning. She would have to contribute to the war effort somehow.

One day a notice on the university bulletin board caught her eye. The Red Cross needed nurses. Edith excitedly scribbled down the information.

"Edith, I absolutely forbid you to do this!" Mama exclaimed, expecting her decision to end the discussion.

"But, Mama, nurses are essential. There are many casualties. Someone has to be concerned!"

"Everyone is concerned, young lady," Mama reminded. "But, I don't want you to become one of the casualties."

"I can take care of myself, Mama," Edith retorted. "Nothing will happen. You'll see. Other girls from the university are already there."

"Darling," Mama insisted, "the others are not my concern. You are! I would be worried sick about you. And what about the Greek examination? You've been studying for months."

"I've asked to have it postponed."

"Will they postpone it?"

"Yes. Very reluctantly."

"Edith, are you ready for the conditions you'll find? Not only will you see horrible wounds, but those hospitals are overrun by *lice*." Mama knew how Edith hated insects. This would clinch the argument. She was pleased to see her daughter shudder at the mention of lice. But the victory instantly slipped away. "I'll face whatever I have to face in the hospitals, Mama," Edith quietly replied.

"All right! I forbid you to go! I won't give my permission." Mama banged her hand firmly on the table.

"Well, then, Mama, I'll go without it!" declared Edith defiantly.

What could poor Frau Stein do? This stubborn girl was truly more like her than any of the other children. If Edith was to go through with this unfortunate plan, the least Frau Stein could do was outfit her with the uniform and supplies she would need. *May God protect her and make her stubbornly good*, Mama prayed.

6

CHOCOLATES AND ORANGES

One thing Edith had avoided mentioning to her mother was that the hospital she was going to was actually a lazzaretto, a hospital for contagious diseases. This lazzaretto, about sixty miles from Breslau, was set up in a converted horse stable. Edith's first assignment was the typhoid ward, where the poor wounded men not only suffered from this painful disease, but often developed pneumonia or other complications.

She hadn't imagined how difficult nursing was going to be. Here she was, a student, bending over broken bodies instead of books. The difficulty wasn't really with the hard work, but with the suffering of the soldiers. In the beginning, she had been assigned to various wards caring for dozens of lonely and suffering men. Now she had to work with those more seriously injured. Among these was a former bricklayer suffering from a very dangerous infection.

"My friend, you must eat to keep up

your strength," Edith implored as she gazed at the listless young man.

"Oh, Nurse, I'm so afraid that I'll die like the others."

"Is there anything...anything at all that you would like to eat?" she asked. "I promise to get it for you."

"Anything at all?" he cried with a forced smile. "Could you perform a magic act and pull an orange out of the air? That's what I'd really like."

A little worried about her promise, Edith made her way to the canteen. To her great surprise, she found a few oranges sitting on one of the shelves. She grabbed one and ran to the bricklayer's bedside.

"Look at this wonderful fruit, my friend. A minor miracle just for you!" The young man was delighted and allowed Edith to feed him the juicy slices.

Later that evening Edith was seated in her room opening a gift package from home. She suddenly bolted from the chair and ran past her startled roommate.

"What in the world did you find in that box? Mice?"

"I'm going back to the ward for a minute," Edith called over her shoulder. "It's Lindt!"

"Lindt?" exclaimed her friend. "Do we have a soldier named Lindt?"

Seconds later Edith was dangling a piece of precious Lindt chocolate over the brick-layer. "Can you stand a second miracle in one day?" she asked teasingly. "This delicious treat will certainly make the medicine go down better, don't you think?"

"Oh, bless your heart, Nurse. You're not just the prettiest girl here...you're an angel!" With that the soldier gobbled up the chocolate like a little boy.

"Let's try to keep a supply of oranges and chocolates for him," Edith told the other nurses. "It may not be what the doctors prescribe, but it will hopefully keep our soldier alive until he can recover."

Always very diligent and energetic about her tasks, Edith spared herself nothing to be of comfort to the ill and injured. She was also very kind to the doctors and nurses. As often as she could, Edith would volunteer for the most distasteful tasks. For example, she gladly served with a particularly nervous nurse simply to give rest to the others. Work was definitely to her liking. Only one thing caused her hesitation. It happened the day she had been assigned to assist a young surgeon in the operating room.

"Nurse, please steady this man's arm while I put the splint on. Good! Now hold it tight for a few moments." With this directive, the doctor placed his own hand firmly on Edith's. She cringed. She wanted to pull away, but this would have pained the injured soldier.

"There were so many patients waiting in that room that I couldn't say anything at the moment, but I gave him such a look," Edith recalled as she reported the disturbing incident to her supervisor. "I'd like a private meeting of the three of us tomorrow, so that I can give him a piece of my mind. You know, we're here to care for these poor soldiers, but that particular doctor is always pushing himself on the nurses."

The next day the doctor stood before Edith as she made her point. "I expect in the future that you will treat me with respect. If you cannot, please stay away from me all together." From that day on the doctor was very courteous toward Edith. She was relieved. Her supervisor could only admire the young woman for standing up for her rights.

7

LAST DANCE

This year of nursing was a time of growth, as well as service, for Edith. She no longer considered it important to always be right. "Even though I could pick out the faults of others very easily, I no longer used this talent to hurt them. Now my goal was to protect them and to be helpful," she admitted. "Telling people the truth about themselves doesn't necessarily make them better. We all have to want to improve. It's like giving permission to others to correct us. It's all in our attitude. We must be kind and accept advice as a kindness. This was my strategy regarding my future brother-in-law, Hans Biberstein, and his mother. Their ways were so different from the ways of my family. The friction and fighting almost caused Erna and Hans to break up. But by patiently trying to understand them, I was able to help my sister Erna adjust better after her wedding."

In fact, Edith put so much effort into the wedding preparations that she was exhausted on the day of the ceremony. While the others were busy setting up chairs in the parlor, Edith was upstairs with a terrible headache. Not wanting her younger sister to miss such an important event, Erna insisted that Edith take some medication. By evening she was feeling fine again.

The wedding and the meal had been perfect. Now there was just the family relaxing together with the newlyweds. The piano began to play a popular new song. Edith turned to Hans and asked mischievously, "Isn't that the dance step you just taught us?"

"It certainly is, Edith. Would you like to join me?" In an instant the two were swinging and swaying to the amusement of all the relatives. Just as Edith and Hans turned to sit down, a waltz began. He made a sweeping bow and reached for Edith's hand. "Well, now we have to prove that we can also dance elegantly." With this they swirled around and around again, delighting their audience.

"I'm glad you seem to be feeling better, Edith," said her new brother-in-law. "I wanted to ask you to dance earlier, since you've always been my star pupil."

Ah, thought Edith as she smiled her thanks, *that was when I was younger. Now that*

"Now we'll show them how elegantly we waltz."

you and Erna are finally married, I can turn my full attention to my own life's journey.

In the serious years ahead, Edith would look back and realize that this was the last time she had ever danced.

"I'm so glad you've decided to come back home, Edith," Frau Stein whispered warmly as she hugged her youngest daughter. "I want you to spend some time resting before you even consider what will come next."

"Yes, Mama. This is just a leave from the Red Cross, but I'm looking forward to being here and enjoying the family. Maybe I'll do some reading and get in touch with a few of my old friends. I'd also like to write to some of my classmates who are still away at war, get together some family entertainment and take some long walks…."

"Maybe a little housework would be relaxing, too," Rosa put in teasingly.

"No work, Rosa," Mama immediately replied. "Edith is to rest. You can see she's tired."

Alone now in her room, Edith began to go over her options. Before leaving Gottingen to join the Red Cross, she had taken the required examinations in history, philosophy and German, and passed with very high marks. Now she had to prepare for the postponed Greek exam. Soon the hospital would be recalling her, too. *Maybe I could take advantage of my experience at the lazzaretto and make a career of nursing,* she thought. *Maybe….*

8

THE OTHER SIDE OF THE DESK

"Teach at Viktoriaschule? My old high school?" Edith was stunned. She was still on leave from the Red Cross, when an urgent invitation arrived. It was from Professor Lengert, her former teacher, and the acting principal at Viktoriaschule. Could she please meet with him? Edith had assumed that one of the students was in need of tutoring. She had so often been called upon to help someone keep up with class work. Now here was the professor begging her to take over as Latin teacher.

"But, Herr Lengert," she protested, "I'm not certified to teach. I've never been in front of a class before."

The professor just stood there with a wry little smile forming beneath his whiskers. "Dear, dear Fraulein Stein, I've never known you to be at a loss," he chuckled. "You'll figure out what to do. I'm sure of it." Becoming more serious he confided, "All of our regular teachers are at the war front, as you know. Right now we have only those called back from retirement, and the sick. I need you to replace young Herr Kretschmar who must go away for some medical treatment. Please don't refuse me, Fraulein."

What could Edith say? At that very moment, she became a teacher. She began with the upper classes of Latin, as well as a few additional classes of German, history and geography. The class load nearly doubled the next semester. Despite her initial attempts to excuse herself as unqualified, Edith attacked this new challenge with her characteristic energy and cleverness. She modeled her classes on those of her own favorite teachers. Her lively enthusiasm for the material rubbed off on her students. Soon they were eagerly delving into a new selection of Latin authors, even tackling some Greek philosophy to better understand Cicero.

"All in all, things are going very well, Mama," Edith said suppressing a yawn. "The principal has given me great freedom in my classes. The students, their parents and the examiners are all pleased with our progress. I'm enjoying myself. I really am. *That* is the only difficulty," she said pointing to the small clock on her desk.

"It's late, darling. Come!" Mama extended her hand as if to lead a naughty child off to bed. She was content with this arrangement. Edith was acquiring a good reputation as a fine teacher.

"Now, Mama, you know the agreement was that I continue working on my doctoral thesis for Professor Husserl along with my teaching. I'm just finishing up this section." In a whisper she added, "Then I'll prepare tomorrow's classes and hop right into bed."

Mama Stein hesitated a moment as if searching for a more convincing argument. Instead she stepped into the room, leaned over and gave Edith a kiss. "I don't like to leave you here alone," she said, shaking her head.

Edith laughingly reassured her as she turned back to her work. "I have Rosa's cookies here to keep me company, Mama. Good night."

Despite her good intentions, Edith really couldn't continue dividing her attention between her research and writing and the class work for the Viktoriaschule. So during the Easter vacation in 1916, she dictated her doctoral dissertation to a small army of three typists. Then she had it bound and shipped off to Professor Husserl, who was now head of the philosophy department at Frieburg University. That summer she handed in her resignation and prepared to make the long trip to Frieburg to discuss her work with Professor Husserl.

What a disappointment awaited her! Husserl had not even read her paper. He explained that at a new university it was expected that he prepare new lectures. This had taken up all his time. "However, Fraulein Stein will attend my course," he said matter-of-factly, "and we will go ahead from there." Frau Husserl and Edith looked at each other in total disbelief, but there was no arguing with the Master.

That month was spent studying for the doctoral examination and attending Husserl's lectures. Edith was joined by a friend, Erika Gothe, who made it her mission that summer to make sure Edith took time to relax. They made quick visits to the Black Forest where they sat with their books, surrounded by the beauty and freshness of nature.

Things began to look up when Professor Husserl read Edith's dissertation. He even spoke to the other professors about "the very original work of Fraulein Stein." One day as Edith and Herr and Frau Husserl were leaving the university together, he turned to her and said, "You know, Edith, you're very talented. I'm thinking of publishing your dissertation in the next issue of the Yearbook. My only reservation is that you've undone several of my theories."

Realizing that she was standing there with her mouth open, Edith tried to take advantage of such a pleasant surprise. "Professor, if you really feel that way about my work, could I stay here in Frieburg and help you?"

Now it was the professor's turn to be surprised. "Would you really consider doing that?" He began stroking his graying goatee excitedly. His thoughts raced through the possibilities of what could be accomplished with such a talented assistant.

Edith did receive her doctorate in philosophy *summa cum laude* (with the highest possible honors) on March 30, 1917. However, she was soon disappointed with her position as Professor Husserl's assistant. Mounds of notes were sorted, edited, catalogued, and presented to the Master for his inspection. Time passed and the Master always had brilliant new insights and theories, but he never seemed to have the time to supervise or approve Edith's work. *This is frustrating because it's for his benefit, after all,* Edith complained to herself.

Then suddenly another event captured her attention.

9

ANOTHER MOTHER

How could I say I won't come? Edith thought, although she wasn't looking forward to returning to the home of her former teacher and friend, Adolf Reinach. Adolf had been one of the most brilliant students of Professor Husserl. It was taken for granted that one day he would replace the great teacher. Now Adolf was dead. *Such a tragic waste of this terrible war,* mused Edith.

Anna, Adolph's young widow, had asked Edith to come and put his philosophical writings in order. Edith, who thought of herself as an atheist, had imagined that she would find Anna overcome by grief. Their time together would be a trial of sorrowful memories. Now as she walked away from the Reinach home, Edith whispered into the crisp afternoon air, "Thank you, Anna. You have shown me the power of hope." Indeed, the new widow radiated love for the cross of Christ, the cross lived out in her own loss. *If the cross can have such power in one woman's life,* thought Edith, *imagine what strength, what comfort must exist in the Church of the cross! It's all so attractive to my poor unbelieving heart.*

The strength of Anna Reinach's Christian faith, as well as the lectures on religion by another friend, Max Scheler, which Edith had so faithfully attended, prepared her for another encounter with Christ.

Books had always been Edith's favored companions. They were her teachers, her friends. They accompanied her everywhere, not just novels, but books of philosophy, history or literature. Now she was face to face with a whole wall of books. This weekend was to be a holiday at the home of her good friend, Hedwig Conrad-Martius, or Hatti, as she was called. However, moments ago Hatti had opened the front door and promptly announced that she and her husband Theodor had to be out of town for two days. Seeing Edith's face drop at the news, Hatti had assured her, "You won't be alone, Edith." Grabbing her arm, she swung her friend around to face the bookcases. "There are so many old and new friends here on the shelves." Then she teasingly added, "Look at how eager they are to be your chosen companions this weekend."

At that moment Theodor, holding a small suitcase in one hand, burst into the room. Without missing a step, he grabbed his wife's arm and pulled her along toward the door. "Sorry to be abandoning you, Edith, but we must be off," he called.

Hatti's laughing voice echoed up from the stairs, "Make yourself at home, Edith. There's food in the pantry. We'll see you tomorrow night." The door slammed shut.

"Well, that was a surprise!" Edith mumbled with a shrug. She turned to the shelves. There were so many of her favorite authors to choose from. *But I'd like to meet someone new tonight*, she decided as she began scanning the titles before her. *What's this?* She pulled off a large volume with the fascinating title, *The Life of Saint Teresa of Jesus, written by herself.* Edith dropped into a chair and began to read. Page after page, she was drawn further into the life of the great Spanish mystic. She read into dusk and darkness. She read into the wee hours of the morning. She read without stopping—all through the night. As the first rays of the morning light crept into the room, she closed the book and hugged it to herself. "This," she murmured, "is certainly the truth." The philosophy she had studied for so many years had never been as convincing as the writing of this sixteenth-century Spanish nun, who would become the mother of a new spiritual life for Edith. Now there could be no turning from the brilliant light of truth she saw in Christ. She longed to know and love him as Saint Teresa had. She had to become a Catholic. "A Catholic *and* a Carmelite," she heard herself say.

After a quick breakfast, Edith hurried into town and bought a catechism and a missal. She pored over them all that day. Soon after this she attended Mass for the first time and presented herself to the priest for baptism. The astonished priest said she would first need to attend some classes on the Catholic faith.

"Father," Edith responded anxiously, "just test me."

He did and was astounded by her knowledge and understanding.

Edith was baptized and received first Holy Communion at Saint Martin's Parish in Bergzabern on New Year's Day, 1922. In the midst of her joy, however, she realized the sorrow her baptism would cause her mother. It would be heartless and cowardly to announce her conversion simply through a letter. No, she had to find a way to gently break the news in person.

"Mama, I'm a Catholic."

Impossible, she gasped to herself. *How could I have just blurted it out like that after all my careful planning?* Edith was kneeling before her sobbing mother. She had just done the one thing she had always feared doing. She had just broken her poor Mama's heart.

10

THE INTERVIEW

After her conversion to Catholicism, Edith felt certain that she was called to become a nun. Her family, however, was still stunned by her decision to convert from their Jewish faith. Edith decided to let some time pass before mentioning the convent to them.

Yet try as she might, it was impossible to obtain a teaching position at a university. This was partly because she was a woman, but especially because she was a Jew. Hitler and his Nazi party were systematically pushing the Jews out of any influential positions in German society. Because of this her spiritual director suggested, "Well, if not a professor at the university, perhaps an instructor at the teachers' college."

So Edith accepted a position at the Dominican Teacher's College in the city of Speyer. Here she lived with the sisters and, in fact, privately took the same vows of chastity, obedience, and poverty. When she wasn't teaching, she worked at translating the theology of Saint Thomas Aquinas into German. She took special joy in being able to help others in hidden acts of kindness and by means of the many letters she wrote.

The students soon grew to respect their new teacher. They were awed by her scholastic achievements and yet attracted by her kindness and attentiveness. Although her favorite hours of the day were those she could spend praying, Edith also made herself available during her free time and often accompanied the young women on their outings.

"The Fraulein Doctor is alone!" Lotte whispered. "If we aren't quick, someone else will get to her first."

"You know," Gretta added, "if she didn't pull her hair back so tightly, I think she would actually be beautiful. She has such expressive eyes. And I just love that dimple on her chin."

"Come on, Gretta. Don't be afraid. Let's ask her."

"I don't want to offend her. She's so straight and proper."

The students grew to respect their new teacher.

"We're going over right now," stated Lotte as she pulled along her reluctant friend.

Plopping down one on either side of their teacher, the girls were almost unnoticed by Edith, who was intently watching a foot race. Encouraged by her little smile and nod of greeting, the two began.

"Fraulein Stein, what do you think of marriage?" Lotte burst out. "I mean, do you think it would be more beneficial for society to dedicate my...ah, our lives to the advancement of women?"

"Is this an interview, ladies?"

"Well, yes, in a way, Fraulein," admitted Gretta.

"*Views on marriage by Professor Edith Stein*.... Are you taking notes?" Edith sweetly asked while pretending to frown.

The girls giggled and nervously smoothed their skirts.

"Well," Edith began, "we've studied marriage in the light of Church teaching...."

"Yes, yes," Lotte interrupted, "but what about your own thoughts...if you don't mind sharing them, that is. Did you ever?..."

"Did I ever think of getting married? Don't all young ladies dream of such things?"

At this the girls eagerly leaned forward. Edith smiled. "Believe it or not, ladies, I was engaged for a while."

"Oh?" gasped the two, exchanging looks of excitement.

"Yes, for a couple of years, in fact. He was very handsome and intelligent..." Edith paused to see the effect of her revelation. "Unfortunately, he was my little nephew, Helmut."

"Oh..." the girls groaned.

"You can't be serious, Fraulein!" Lotte exclaimed.

"I had been nurse to the little fellow not long before. And you know how many romances arise from that kind of relationship," Edith continued maliciously. "My lucky day came at my sister's engagement party. Little Helmut whispered in my ear: 'Aunt Edith, will you be my bride?' 'Of course,' I replied. We then shared a piece of cake, as is proper for the engaged couple. Do you know that we kept up this little fantasy for several years. He very reluctantly gave it up after much teasing from the relatives."

"But weren't there ever any *real* boy friends?" the two begged.

"Now, do you doubt that there were?" Edith mischievously responded. "You wouldn't want me to be publicizing these things, would you? What would that do to my present chances?" With that Edith got up and walked off, smiling to herself.

Later that day as she was reflecting on the questions of Lotte and Gretta, Edith recalled a certain young man at school. Yes, for a while she had considered him a "very desirable life partner." Earlier there had been the obvious attention of her cousin, Franz. More recently, there had been Hans Lipps, a fellow philosopher, who had actually asked her to marry him. However, her reply to him was, "It's too late."

Edith greatly respected, and perhaps even loved Hans, but at her baptism, she felt a call to contemplative life, the life of Carmel. Jesus had claimed her heart already, it was too late to consider marriage.

"Dear Jesus," she prayed. "How much longer will it be before I can come to Carmel? All I want is a life hidden in you."

11

A JOYFUL YES

For a time Edith was much sought after as a lecturer. She traveled around Germany and even gave talks in Paris, Vienna, Prague, Basel and Salzburg. She stressed the issue of women's rights, the dangers of anti-religious sentiments, and the nobility and vocation of each human person. She was very effective, but soon enough even these opportunities were cut short by government pressure.

Edith saw this as a clear sign that it was time to seek entrance to Carmel. Her spiritual director agreed. But would the Carmelite nuns accept her? Edith asked advice of a friend who knew the Carmelites of Cologne-Lindenthal. Together the two of them went to present her request, but it was her friend who had the first interview. Because of the convent schedule, Edith herself had to return in the afternoon. Needless to say, she was back in the chapel long before the nuns sang Vespers. She joined in all the afternoon prayers. At three-thirty, she found herself in the parlor, facing Mother Josepha, the prioress, and Mother Teresa Renata, the novice mistress.

"Yes, this has been the desire of my heart since I received baptism, almost twelve years ago." Edith anxiously answered all the questions put to her.

"I lived with the Dominican Sisters at Speyer for eight years while I taught in their school, and I have often visited the Abbey at Beuron, but I never felt attracted to either community. I feel very strongly that there is something special awaiting me at Carmel."

Mother Renata expressed her only reservation. "I wonder if it would be right to take from the world a woman who still has so much to offer intellectually?"

Edith's reply startled the nuns. "It's not human activity that can help us, Mother, but only the Passion of Christ. I desire a share in that."

The two Carmelites were pleased with what they observed of Doctor Stein. She appeared to be humble and sincere. However, they concluded, she would have to seek an interview with the Father Provincial who would be visiting soon.

Edith boarded the train and returned to Munster, where she was living at that time.

It was Pentecost so she spent her days at prayer in the cathedral imploring the Holy Spirit for a favorable reply. After all, it was asking a lot of the Carmelites to accept her, considering that she was forty-two years old, had nothing to offer as a dowry, "and that I am Jewish." Encouraged by her prayer, she wrote a note explaining to the nuns that she needed their answer immediately because her situation was so insecure.

They did understand. She was invited to return and to meet all of the nuns. This time Edith found herself seated at the grille facing the whole community. They were very kind and attentive, and very curious to hear about the famous liturgies at the Benedictine Abbey of Beuron, where she frequently attended Mass.

Now it was Edith's turn to be surprised. Would she sing a little song, the nuns asked? It was customary for those seeking admission to the community, they explained.

Softly, shyly, she sang a simple little Marian hymn. "Oh!" she gasped when it was over, "that was more frightening than speaking before a thousand people!" Her meaning was lost on all but Mother Josepha and Mother Renata. The others had no idea of her past experiences. With relief Edith realized that none of these holy women knew of her reputation. All they saw was a new candidate eager to share in their life of simplicity and prayer. As she was leaving, she was told that the community would vote the next day. A telegram would announce their decision.

After a long restless night, the telegram came. She drank in the simple words: "Joyful acceptance. Greetings. Carmel." It was June 19, 1933.

After she concluded her commitments in Munster, Edith spent a month in the Carmel guesthouse. It was a wonderful month in which she came to know better this new life which she wished with all her heart to embrace. Her belongings were transferred to the monastery. She possessed very little aside from the six cartons of theology and philosophy books. Now she had only one thing left to do. And it would be the hardest thing she had ever done.

12

THE SORROWFUL MOTHER

The sign on the platform announced that her train was pulling into Breslau, her hometown. Edith was not to enter the Carmel of Cologne-Lindenthal until the feast of Saint Teresa of Avila on October 15. So there would be time to prepare her family for the news of her decision. So far, she had only written to say that she had found a place to stay with some sisters in Cologne and would be moving there permanently in October. Her family assumed that she had found a new teaching assignment in Cologne.

Collecting her two small bags, Edith stepped off the train. *What a relief*, she thought, *Rosa came alone to meet me*. Rosa was the only member of Edith's immediate family who sympathized with her conversion. She also felt drawn to Jesus, but had not requested baptism out of respect for their mother.

"Edith, Edith," she called. "What a nice surprise to have you home!" Noticing the look on Edith's face, she dropped the bag she had just picked up and stared at her sister. "What is it? Are you ill?"

"No, Rosa. I'm very well, but there is something I must tell you before we go home. I'm telling you because I know you'll understand."

"What, Edith? What won't wait until we're home with Mama?"

"I'm going to become a Carmelite nun. I've already been accepted," Edith said all in one breath.

Rosa closed her eyes and nodded. She hadn't expected this, but she wasn't surprised. It made perfect sense when you knew Edith and...and when you knew Jesus.

"I beg you, Rosa, don't speak a word of this to Mama or to any of the others. Will you promise?"

"I promise, Edith. I promise and I'll be praying."

No one else asked Edith anything about her new position except her very observant nephew Wolfgang, who was now twenty-one. He, too, promised to keep her secret. In this way the weeks went on in peace. Erna and Hans Biberstein were moving from the apartment in the Stein house to the other side of town to be nearer to Erna's new medical practice. Helping them pack and transfer their belongings was a relaxing task for Edith...until one day, Erna finally asked about Cologne. The two sisters were standing side by side in the trolley car when it happened.

"I'm entering the Carmelite monastery in Cologne," Edith quietly admitted.

Erna stood there with tears welling up in her eyes. It seemed like forever to Edith before her sister let out a long exasperated sigh. "You've always been so stubborn," Erna choked as if drowning in her stifled tears. "You do and then you think. Just like the summer before Hans and I married. Remember?" Erna was making a valiant effort to lighten the situation. "We had hiked all over the mountains and then came to the hotel to find no rooms were available. And you—you parked yourself, sprained ankle and all, in the dining room and stared down that poor clerk. 'I'm not leaving until you give us rooms!' you said. We were mortified, but you did get us rooms. You've always been so strong-headed!" Erna paused to collect herself. "And now," she continued, "you insist on entering a convent. Carmel, of all places! Oh, Edie, if you can't think of how this hurts us, can't you have pity on Mama? You know how she loves you. You're her favorite; we all admit it."

Uncomfortable at this remark, Edith made a sign as if to brush it off.

"It's true Edith, you *are* the favorite of all of us. That's why this news hurts so much. It was hard enough on the family when you became a Catholic, but this, too?" After a few moments, she concluded in disgust, "Life is dreadful. What brings happiness to one person causes such pain to others."

Edith turned abruptly toward the window, pretending to search for the next street sign. She fought to hold back her tears.

A few days later Erna took her sister aside. "Hans would like you to come and stay with us, Edith," she said with a note of hope in her voice. "He believes your decision is due to some financial difficulty. I know that's never been a factor in your choices, but I promised him I would speak to you."

"Thank Hans for me, Erna," Edith smiled gratefully. "Thank you both for trying to understand me. But I must follow my vocation. Remember, the convent will never make you less dear to me."

Now Edith's constant preoccupation was her mother. How would she break the news? Several days later they were alone in the house, just Edith and her mother. Suddenly Frau Stein looked up from her knitting. "What will you be doing with the sisters in Cologne?" she asked.

The dreaded moment had arrived. Although trembling inside, Edith gazed steadily into her mother's eyes. "I will live with them, Mama," she softly replied.

Frau Stein understood what Edith left unsaid. The happiness that had filled the cozy room just moments before was shattered. A wedge of pain had suddenly come between them. Mama tried to maintain her self-control, but her hands began to shake and her yarn became hopelessly tangled. The moment remained frozen in time.

Edith had just added one more worry on the dear old woman, and this realization weighed heavily on her. She knew that although her mother was an intelligent businesswoman who still maintained control over her lumberyard, she had financial troubles. Times were hard, especially within the Jewish community. It was becoming more difficult to obtain lumber and to retain the loyalty of her customers. Besides this, there was now the empty apartment in the family home. Since the Bibersteins had moved out, many people had come to look at it, but no one had come near to signing a rental agreement.

Among the interested parties had been a particular Protestant congregation. One day three of the ministers came to take a second look at the rooms. Frau Stein asked Edith to take them through. She managed to get them to agree on terms. However, after a few days, they began to waver. This would never do. Edith went to call on the head pastor.

"I am sorry, Fraulein. I understand your impatience to settle this matter, but we are undecided. Please don't look so sad."

"Forgive me, sir, for seeming so impertinent, but I am concerned to leave my mother with so many sorrows," Edith said.

"What is it that weighs the poor woman down?" the minister inquired with obvious concern.

"Well, besides the house, there is my conversion to Catholicism, and now my decision to enter the Carmel of Cologne-Lindenthal," Edith explained. "I'm her youngest daughter and she feels this very deeply. She is a fervent Jew and this is all just bewildering to her. I'm sure you can understand."

The good man was deeply moved by Edith's revelation and promised to do his utmost to close the deal quickly. He left with another promise, "I want you to know, dear Fraulein Stein, that regarding your decision, you have found a sympathetic heart in me."

But there were no sympathetic hearts at home. Even Rosa found it hard to understand how Edith could inflict this suffering on their mother. The question kept arising. Twelve-year-old Susel Biberstein pleaded, "But why, Aunt Edith? Why now? Don't you see how it looks to everyone? It looks as if you're running away!"

Susel's father, Hans, also came in person to present the same argument. "Edith, I know you well enough to realize that nothing I say can change your mind. These are dangerous times, but you can't pretend that you are no longer a Jew!"

Edith wasn't running away. And she certainly wasn't trying to pretend she was no longer a Jew. These misunderstandings and accusations hurt her deeply. They caused her to place even more trust in the Lord who was calling her to a life, not of escape, but of greater nearness to the people he had chosen. In this darkness, she often looked at her mother, who suffered so silently, and wondered, *Who will break first under this strain, you or me?*

The last day of the Jewish Feast of Tabernacles, October 12, 1933, was also Edith's birthday. There would be no party this year. It was her last day at home. It was also the Day of Atonement for the Jews.

Despite her age, Frau Stein had insisted that they should walk home from the synagogue after the feast day observance. Both mother and daughter were thinking over their earlier conversation. Edith had reminded her mother that the first few months at Carmel would be only a trial period. If it didn't work out....

"You offer me no consolation," Mama had broken in. "I know my daughter too well. If you take on a time of probation, I know you'll pass."

Now as they walked by all those familiar houses, Frau Stein looked at Edith and eagerly prodded, "Don't you think the rabbi gave a fine sermon?"

"He did, Mama."

"So, then, you agree that one can be devout as a Jew?"

"Of course, Mama, if one has known only that," Edith gently replied.

"Then why did you have to know anything else, Edith? Why?" the older woman desperately cried. "I don't want to speak against *him*. Jesus was probably a very good man. But I don't understand why he had to make himself God!"

Edith couldn't answer. By now, they had arrived home at their street, Michaelis-strasse. Edith took her mother's arm as they crossed it and entered the house.

There was a constant coming and going of family and friends that day. It helped to ease the pain. But after supper that evening, Edith and her mother remained at table facing each other. In their heart of hearts each was praying, *O God, when will I ever touch this dear face again?* And they cried.

The next morning when Edith came home from early Mass at Saint Michael's Church, she found the whole family gathered for breakfast. Her mother tried to eat something, but after a few bites she pushed the dish away and began to cry. Edith got up from her place and went around behind her mother's chair. She put her arms around her and held her close to her heart. Time was ticking away. The train for Cologne would be leaving at eight o'clock. Edith signaled to Erna to come over and take her place by their mother.

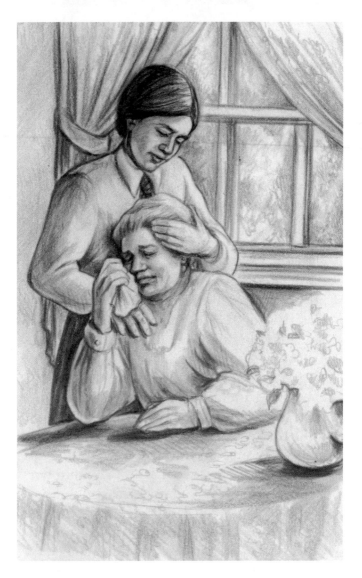

Frau Stein began to weep loudly.

Edith left for a moment and returned dressed in her hat and coat. Mother and daughter warmly embraced and kissed. But when Edith went to embrace Erna, Frau Stein began to weep loudly. Edith left quickly.

Only her older sisters, Else and Rosa, accompanied her to the train station. She noticed from her place in the train that while Else was upset, Rosa was so calm and peaceful it seemed that she too was on her way to Carmel.

13

THE HOUSE OF THE LORD

Finally, finally, finally! thought Edith. With a joyful heart she stepped into the cloister of Carmel. She heard the heavy door lock behind her. The vocation of the Discalced Carmelite is not easy. It rejoices the heart of one who is called, but it is a stark, no frills religious life. There are long, intense periods of prayer, an absolute simplicity of lifestyle, a strict poverty, a spirit of childlike humility. How would a famous philosopher, now over forty-two years of age and used to esteem and praise, to freedom and possessions, adapt herself to these new circumstances? Edith didn't stop to study how, she just gave herself completely to the love of the Lord. She knew that this was where she belonged. And she blossomed as a flower in the desert.

Long before her arrival at Carmel, Edith had realized that the cross awaited her in some unknown form. She embraced this unseen participation in the Lord's Passion. Some may have thought that this cross came in her inability to perform the tiniest house-keeping tasks. She had spent her years as a student and later a teacher, and had never been asked to cook or clean. Her sewing was a disaster. But Edith didn't see the promised cross in these humiliations. They were just part of the schooling necessary for one whose whole life had been marked by accomplishment and praise. Her good humor and patience in her new role made her loved by the whole community. Doctor Edith Stein became a spiritual child in the hands of her superiors and a joyful, attentive companion to her sisters.

"She was a marvelous story-teller who could make an adventure of the smallest details. She delighted us with her witty remarks and inspired us by her piety," attested Mother Renata. "Never did she let on what her life had been before entering. She never made anyone feel inferior to her in any way."

When the six-month probationary period was over, Edith was joyfully admitted to the novitiate. Just as her mother had predicted, she had passed the test.

Good Shepherd Sunday, April 15, 1934, was the day designated for Edith's entrance into this next step in her religious life. She came forward to receive the heavy brown Carmelite habit. She was dressed in a glowing white bridal gown made from material Rosa had sent. The chapel was filled with flowers and friends. Many priests and religious were present, along with quite a few of her fellow students. The main celebrant was none other than the Benedictine Abbot of Beuron. Radiant and attentive, Edith answered the ancient Carmelite dialogue:

"What do you ask?"

"God's mercy, the poverty of Carmel and the company of my sisters."

"Are you resolved to persevere in Carmel until your death?"

"This is my hope and desire, with God's grace and the prayers of the sisters."

Edith knelt before the cross and kissed it. She was then led out and clothed in the Carmelite habit. Coarse rope sandals replaced her shoes, and a leather belt was put around her waist. A full-length garment called a scapular was placed over her shoulders. Finally, the crown of flowers she had been wearing was replaced with a white veil. The ceremony was complete. Edith now prostrated herself in the form of a cross before the altar. Her friends and family no longer saw before them their illustrious doctor of philosophy, the tireless seeker of wisdom, but the future spouse of the Eternal Truth, Sister Teresa Benedicta of the Cross.

Photographs of the day were shown to Professor Husserl who had been unable to attend. Those present say that he joked, "I should have been there as a proud father to give her away." Although his famous student had parted from some of his teachings, he was very pleased to call her the greatest of the Church's new philosophers.

Sister Benedicta would have been satisfied to leave her intellectual pursuits forever. However, the Father Provincial took the opportunity of her clothing ceremony to interview the new sister about her former activities. He was impressed and made her take out of storage a work she had been unable to complete. She was to be relieved of all other duties. Her main occupation would be to write. And so, in the midst of the holy routine of prayer and community, Sister Benedicta again took up her pen. She finished her translation of Saint Thomas' great work. She also found time to write many biographical sketches of famous Carmelite figures and even prepared a number of skits for the enjoyment of the sisters. For relaxation between her more serious endeavors, she began to write her own story, which she entitled *Life in a Jewish Family*. Unfortunately, she was never able to finish it. Some believe that her greatest book, *The Science of the Cross*, was never completed either.

14

Bride of the Lamb

Although the Carmelites celebrate the reception of the habit in a ceremony open to friends and family, the day of profession of vows is a private affair. In the pre-dawn hours of the morning of Easter 1935, the community filed into choir, the monastery chapel reserved for the nuns alone. The fragrant aroma of flowers mingled with the familiar scent of melting wax. No one was present in the adjoining public chapel. The priest had not yet arrived for Mass.

After the first Alleluias were sung, Sister Benedicta knelt and placed her hands between those of the prioress. With a jubilant heart, she began, "I, Sister Teresa Benedicta of the Cross, profess...." With that sacred promise Sister Benedicta offered her life to her beloved Jesus. This was a temporary profession for only three years, but to her it was a lifetime pledge of love. She would gladly promise her chastity, poverty, and obedience before Our Lady of Mount Carmel and in the hands of the prioress. She would wholeheartedly live the rule and constitutions of the Order of Discalced Carmelites. This moment of joy would last a lifetime and sustain her in the moments of suffering ahead.

Sister Benedicta stepped out into the garden. It was like a fairyland. Every tree was an explosion of blossoms. *Especially the myrtle,* she thought. *They are so like cascades of clouds hanging down into our very own yard. The fluffy, light, lovely clouds of heaven peeking in on our celebration. How appropriate! From this moment on, I am pledged to heaven. I am to be like the great prophet Elijah, always standing before the face of God, always interceding for the cares of those beyond this beautiful spot.... Ah, and now for a photograph of the happy bride!*

"Sister Benedicta, please stand on the path over there. Good! Just a step to the left. Fine. Now hold still.... Oh, could you straighten the rose crown a bit? Beautiful! Here we go."

Yes, the photograph always becomes the many photographs. But they will make so many others happy. I must be patient. I don't need them myself.... I am the Bride of the Lamb! Perhaps I will burst from happiness.

"You can relax now, Sister Benedicta. I'm finished."

"Thank you. God bless you!" *I can relax now! How true! I feel a bit guilty. The Lord is treating me like a favorite child. I know I will have to grow up soon. Jesus, the Paschal Lamb, will also invite me to celebrate the sacrifice. But he will give me the grace when the time comes. Today he requires only rejoicing from his bride.*

"Sister Benedicta! Sister Benedicta!" called one of the sisters. "Come in. We're waiting for you!"

"I'm coming!" Sister Benedicta spun around one more time as if to inhale the garden splendor. *I am coming, Lord. Thank you for the springtime. Whenever I see the beauties of this season, it will remind me of this holy day.*

Those who visited Sister Benedicta after her profession day said that she seemed to have lost at least twenty years. She was so radiant and joyful—a young woman in love. Happiness seemed to surround her. She had found complete peace and contentment in her hidden life of prayer and sacrifice.

"Now that you're a professed Carmelite, Sister Benedicta, you'll no longer have to worry about your future," one friend assured her. To the woman's surprise, Sister Benedicta replied solemnly, "I'm afraid that will not be the case. They will surely pursue me even here." It was obvious that Sister

Benedicta could clearly read the dangerous moves of the Nazis. She was under no illusions. Suffering with and for her people was written into her destiny.

15

Within the Castle

Saint Teresa of Avila, whose autobiography had inspired Sister Benedicta to enter Carmel, also wrote another book called *The Interior Castle.* This book leads the reader through the steps of the spiritual journey to God. The holy mother of Carmel speaks of the soul as if it were traveling through a castle, passing from one room to another in its search for God. This search became the great adventure that occupied Sister Benedicta's heart. She accepted the Carmelite Rule as a most blessed challenge. As the oldest of the "young" sisters in the community, she was often called upon to explain this holy way to the novices. She was very successful at this, not just because of her ability to simplify difficult concepts, but because it was all so alive in her own person.

Her influence extended beyond the walls of the Carmel of Cologne-Lindenthal. Sister Benedicta carried on a great apostolate through her letters. They were filled with friendship, good advice, warmth, and wit, and were treasured by those who received them. In these letters, she applied her mind to answer problems of philosophy. She gently led friends to belief in Jesus. She kept involved in the affairs of her family. However, the most important letters for her were those that she faithfully sent to her mother. Knowing the uniqueness of her situation, her superiors encouraged her to write home weekly. Yet, despite her dedication to this correspondence, it was years before Frau Stein sent a reply. All news was passed through Rosa. It was a wonderful, welcome surprise when Mama's best wishes first appeared at the bottom of one of Rosa's notes.

"Can you imagine," Sister Benedicta later shared with the nuns, "my mother actually went over to visit the new Carmel in Breslau! You know she's now eighty-seven years old. That was quite an adventure for her. And she went alone. The family had no idea that she had this in mind."

"Perhaps she just decided to see for herself what kind of life you're leading," one of the sisters suggested.

"I'm sure you're right," Sister Benedicta replied. "Whatever the good sisters shared with her has done wonders. I now receive a few lines from her in each of Rosa's letters."

Although Frau Stein was never able to make the trip to Cologne-Lindenthal, she now felt more at peace with her daughter's chosen life. And, in the mysterious ways of God, he arranged for one last visit between these two devoted hearts. It occurred on the Feast of the Exaltation of the Holy Cross, September 14, 1936. In the early hours of this particular feast day, all the Carmelites renew their vows of chastity, poverty and obedience. As Sister Benedicta waited in line for her turn, she suddenly felt the presence of someone next to her. She was both delighted and bewildered to realize that it was her dear mother she felt standing there. *How could this be, Lord?* she wondered.

A few hours later a telegram brought the news that Mama had passed away at the very hour that Sister Benedicta had sensed her presence in choir. How thoughtful was the Lord to allow this last consolation to his bride.

After putting her mother's things in order, there was nothing to keep Rosa from fulfilling her desire to follow her sister into the Catholic Church. First she would visit her. She arrived in Cologne to find that Sister Benedicta was in the hospital. She had missed a step in the dark. Both her left hand and foot were broken. Although this temporarily disabled her, Sister Benedicta considered the pain a blessing. It made it possible for Rosa to come to the hospital every day for last minute instruction. Christmas Day was set as the day of her baptism. Since Sister Benedicta was to be released from the hospital, she was able to attend. Delighted, both sisters considered this an added touch of God's goodness.

In Easter week of 1938, Sister Benedicta made her final vows. Now she would belong to Jesus forever. A black veil replaced her white one. She had finished the years of formation and was now truly at home within the castle of the King of Heaven.

16

THE SHADOW OF THE CROSS

Sister Benedicta had been concentrating on putting her thoughts down on paper. But something was distracting her. It was usually much easier to find the right words. What was troubling her? "Oh, dear Jesus!" she gasped when she allowed her eyes to focus on the paper that lay before her on the desk. The sun shining against her window frame had cast the shadow of the cross right across her work. With her finger she gently traced over the shadow and then reverently signed herself with it. She silently prayed, *Lord, you know all things. You see how your cross comes closer every day. I sit here writing, but no one will publish my work. They offer polite excuses, but I know they are afraid to accept the writings of a Jew. Anti-Semitism is everywhere. You see how frightened my family is by this ugly hatred. Where will it all lead, my Beloved?*

Everyone was taking the German political situation seriously those days. The bishop had even granted the Carmelites permission to leave the cloister in order to go to the polls and vote. They were gathering at the front door in preparation when some men arrived at the gate. To their astonishment, it was the polling officers. The officials were carrying a ballot box with them.

"Gentlemen, excuse our surprise, but this is really unnecessary," Mother Prioress said.

"Now, Mother," they soothed. "Everyone knows you are cloistered here and are not normally allowed to leave the monastery. We thought we would save you the inconvenience of travelling out to the polls."

"Voting is not an inconvenience, gentlemen," Mother insisted. "It is our duty as citizens. We do it gladly. It is also good example to the people."

The argument was useless. The two men sat themselves down and began calling out the sisters' names. They realized, as they went along, that a few sisters had not come forward to vote. "Where is Anna Fitzeck?" they demanded.

"She can't come downstairs. She isn't well today," Mother replied.

"And Doctor Edith Stein? Where is she?"

"She doesn't have the right to vote," Mother answered cautiously.

"Of course she does! It says here that her date of birth is 1891."

Calmly Mother Prioress responded, "Sister is non-Aryan."

The men quickly noted this next to her name and left.

When Sister Benedicta was told what had happened, she insisted that the prioress consider transferring her. "I'm a danger to all of you, Sisters. I must seek refuge in another place. The cross has fallen on our convent. We must heed the sign."

Arrangements were quickly made with the Carmel in Echt, Holland. There were historical ties between the two Carmels. The Carmelites of Cologne had founded the Echt monastery in the late 1800s, during the Kulturkampf—the period of Bismarck's persecution of the Church. The Netherlands were politically neutral. They neither sided with, nor opposed the German Third Reich. It was believed that the Echt monastery would be a safe haven for Sister Benedicta during those difficult times.

It was a very sad moment for Sister Benedicta. She knew this would be a final farewell. She was certain that she would never return to her monastery, nor would she ever see her beloved community again. The departure would be made under cover of darkness. A heroic doctor volunteered to drive her across the border to Echt. It was New Year's Eve, 1938.

The nuns of the Echt community welcomed the newcomer with joy. Soon, despite the necessary adjustments to the routine and customs of this new house, Sister Benedicta settled in. Among her first challenges was the task of learning Dutch. Sister Benedicta made this a priority and very quickly mastered the language, adding it to the growing list of languages that she already knew. Her days soon became a beautiful round of prayer, writing, teaching, and community life.

Among Sister Benedicta's most ardent prayers were those said for the safety of her family. Erna and her family seemed well established in America. Arno also had left Germany. But Else, Paul, Frieda and Rosa were all struggling amid the dangers in their homeland.

In the summer of 1940, one of these worries was turned to joy. After a failed attempt to join a new religious community in Belgium, Rosa made her way to the Carmel of Echt. Here she became a Third Order Carmelite. She lived in a room adjoining the convent and carried out the duties of a lay member of the community. Just as in her mother's home in Breslau, Rosa found her happiness in service. She gladly involved herself with the garden and the external affairs of the monastery. Rosa seemed to possess all the practicality that her sister lacked. She spent her days in caring for the needs of the community and in long hours of prayer.

Both the Stein sisters seemed settled and content. However, word of the escalating violence penetrated even the cloister. Rosa related what she heard in news reports. Friends also wrote about the latest horrors taking place among the Jews. One Sunday as Rosa and Sister Benedicta were visiting together in the parlor, Rosa passed on some frightening news. "You must tell Mother Prioress to have the sisters pray for the Carmelites in Aachen and in Duren. I was told that the Gestapo suddenly attacked both houses and drove the sisters out."

"Oh, Rosa! I'll tell Mother as soon as we go in for Vespers. Those poor sisters!" Sister Benedicta lamented.

"Edith, do you think we're really safe

here? Remember that in February it was the sisters in Luxembourg who were driven out. People tell me that their monastery was turned into a meeting place for some girls' group. How much worse can this get?"

Sister Benedicta became very silent for a few moments. Then looking up at her sister, she replied resolutely, "I'm going to suggest to Mother that you and I apply to the Carmel of Le Paquier in Switzerland. I don't feel we'll be safe here for long."

After being told of the latest violence, the prioress agreed that action must be taken. Letters seeking the various civil and ecclesiastical permissions went out quickly. The answers, however, never seemed to come. There was one difficulty after another. A major problem was that the community of Le Paquier had already turned away several young women who wanted to enter, because there was no more room. Could they now accept Sister Benedicta and Rosa? And what was holding up the visas?

Talk of visas aroused the interest of the occupying German authorities. The sisters were summoned to appear before them. With extraordinary calm, Sister Benedicta greeted the captain of the Gestapo with the traditional form of religious address, "Praised be Jesus Christ!" This momentarily startled the man, but when he looked at her papers and saw that the prescribed "J" was missing, he became furious.

"Where is the mark of the Jew on this identity card, Doctor Stein?" he bellowed. "And the 'Sara' before your name! Where is it? Every Jewish woman is 'Sara!' You must write immediately to Breslau and ask for a new identity card!" He paused a moment for breath. "You must write and 'humbly request' that a new one be issued," he added sarcastically. "Immediately!"

Sister Benedicta admitted that she had left this encounter shaking inside. "Not so much from fear. I know the Lord will provide for us. But that man was like the devil incarnate."

She later made an even more startling confession. "I wear next to my heart a piece of paper with the words of Matthew 10:23, 'If you are persecuted in one town, move on to another one.' The passage continues in the Gospel, 'I promise that you will not have traveled to all the towns of Israel before the Son of Man comes.' This is my consolation. The efforts to move to Le Paquier are progressing so slowly and I'm so absorbed with the writing of *The Science of the Cross*, that I'm actually becoming indifferent. I'm ready for whatever God wills."

17

Revenge!

Sister Benedicta was becoming more and more resigned to whatever lay ahead. The nuns at Le Paquier had finally reached a decision. They had voted to accept the two Stein sisters. Preparations were underway to transport them and to make them comfortable in their new refuge. But the border between Holland and Switzerland was securely bound by red tape. And there were still no visas.

All sorts of restrictions were being leveled on the Jews. They had to wear a bright yellow Star of David on their outer clothing. Jewish children were to be taught only by Jewish teachers. No Jews were allowed to enter public buildings. Accounts began to circulate of mass deportations of large numbers of Jews. Much speculation was afoot about the safety of the many Jewish Catholics who were members of religious congregations. The commissioner assured the local bishop that there was absolutely no reason to be concerned. These Jewish Catholics would not be deported.

Then came a tragic turn of events.

Although they were grateful for the assurance that the Jewish Catholic priests and religious would be left alone, the Dutch bishops decided that they must speak out against the general policy of deportation of the Jews. A pastoral letter condemning this inhuman practice was to be read at every Mass on Sunday, July 26, 1942.

Revenge was sudden and swift. At five o'clock in the afternoon of August 2, there was a knock at the monastery grille.

"Mother, there are officers outside asking for Sister Benedicta."

"Oh, thanks be to God," the prioress said. "It's probably about the travel visas. Call Sister to the grille."

Sister Benedicta went confidently to the grille, only to be confronted by the "SS", officers of the feared secret police.

"Ah, Doctor Stein. You and your sister will accompany us, please."

"Herr Commandant, my title is unnecessary. Here I am only Sister Teresa Benedicta. You can...."

"No formalities. Just come. Quickly!"

"But we are expecting our visas for Switzerland!"

"We'll deal with that later. For now, you are to come with us. Immediately! I give you ten minutes to collect your things and be out on the street," the commandant concluded.

Sister Benedicta hurried back into the enclosure, stopped for a quick prayer in choir, then raced up to her room. All the sisters began bustling around trying to prepare a few things for what they hoped would be a temporary journey.

"This is so frightening, Mother," Sister Benedicta admitted, a bit frazzled by the suddenness of it all. Then seeing the fear on the faces around her, she attempted to sound confident. "I'm sure we'll be back soon, so don't worry. Say a prayer that all goes well,… and contact the Swiss Consul right away. Beg for those visas!"

Rosa was kneeling outside, hoping for a last minute blessing from the prioress. As soon as Sister Benedicta stepped out of the door, the two were hastily escorted to a waiting truck.

All the nuns crowded around the prioress for a last glance at Sister Benedicta and Rosa as they climbed up into the truck. Only as it pulled away did they realize that no one had been able to give a parting hug to either of the sisters.

What was that first day's journey like? Those left behind could only speculate and follow those arrested with their fervent prayers. Three days after the abduction of Sister Benedicta and Rosa, a telegram arrived at Echt. It was a request for warm clothes, blankets and medicines to be sent to a camp in Westerbork. The nuns scoured their meager belongings for things that could be sent. They quickly assembled enough material for several parcels. These were entrusted to two reliable men of Echt.

"Gentlemen, what did you find? How are the sisters?" the prioress breathlessly asked the two messengers when they returned from Westerbork.

"Fortunately, Mother," one reported, "the camp is guarded by Dutch police, so we had no trouble getting in to see Sister Benedicta and Fraulein Rosa."

"And how are they?"

"Will they be back soon?"

"Did they say anything?"

"Slow down, Sisters. One at a time, please," the second man called out. "As we told you, there was no problem entering the camp. Actually, we had no difficulty locating the sisters either, because there is a whole hut of nuns there."

"Yes," the first man joined in, "Sister Benedicta said they are ten in all."

"You saw her then? How is she holding up, sir? Her health is really not that good, you know," broke in one anxious nun.

"Don't worry. She seems quite well and actually very lively. I think she's taken the rest of those nuns under her wing. She said that they're trying to act as a community of sorts. She told us to tell you, Mother, to be at peace in her regard. They have plenty of time for prayer and the food is sufficient. Fraulein Rosa seems in good spirits, too."

"This will please you, Mother," said the other man. "As we were leaving, a Jewish woman came up to us. She had seen us speaking to Sister Benedicta. 'That sister is such a blessing to all of us. She has been everywhere with her kindness, comforting the children, washing them, brushing their hair, making sure they eat. She is truly an angel of charity!'"

"Hush now. I'll be your mother."

The next day a note arrived from Sister Benedicta. She wanted to assure the prioress that she was content. Referring to the book she had been writing when the arrest came, she said, "It is only possible to learn the *Science of the Cross* by living it. I have always been certain of this and repeat it again with all my heart, *Hail, Cross, our only hope!*"

Mother Prioress felt tears well up in her eyes. *You are truly blessed by the cross, my child*, she thought. *May the Lord protect you and bring you back to us.*

Exactly what happened next is lost in history. A small card came to the nuns indicating that the Jewish Catholics were taken from a holding camp and shipped in a freight train to the "East," most likely to the notorious prison camp of Auschwitz. There were several reports later of people who encountered Sister Benedicta on this difficult journey.

A stationmaster told of being surprised when he glanced up and saw a woman dressed in brown standing in the door of the train car. She looked so peaceful amid that crowd of suffering people. She asked only that he give regards from Doctor Edith Stein to the Schwinds, the family of her former spiritual advisor.

At another train station, a young woman was startled to hear someone call out her name. The caller was a woman dressed in brown. She said she was Doctor Stein, the young woman's former teacher. Would the young woman please bring a greeting from her to the Carmelites?

When the train stopped to refuel in Breslau, Sister Benedicta appeared at an opening. She spoke to a mailman who was gaping in horror at the death train. She mentioned that this was her hometown, but that she was going to her death and would never see it again.

"Do your companions know this?" the shocked mailman asked.

"It's better that they don't know," she quietly responded. This occurred on August 7, 1942. It was the last known meeting with Sister Benedicta.

Now they were finally off that terrible train. It had been so dark, so frightening. Yet this place was not much better. They were struggling along, trying to make their aching legs move. The soldiers were roughly pressing them forward.

It was definitely better to be out of that stuffy car, but the air out here wasn't very fresh. It actually tasted bitter…and the smell?… Where were they going?

Sister Benedicta raised her head hoping to catch a glimpse of their destination. It was cloudy up there. And there appeared to be…a kind of glow! They seemed to be headed directly toward some type of furnace. "Beloved Jesus!" she murmured.

Quickly Sister Benedicta lowered her head and grasped more tightly the little hand at her side.

"Does holding my hand make you feel better?" she said as gently as she could.

"Yes," came the tired reply.

"Do you want to know a secret, dear little Edith?"

Anxiously the child answered, "Yes, Sister Benedicta. Please!"

"Live in God's hand. Just as we are holding hands here. Every day we need to reach up and hold God's hand. Let him lead us, or be with us, in whatever happens."

Little Edith squeezed her protector's hand. "Just like this?"

"That's right, dear, just like that. Now, tell me, do you know the Psalms?"

"I know some of them," the little girl whispered.

"Let's say this one together then as we walk: 'God, my Father, though I walk in the darkness, I am not afraid for you are with me....'"

18

LIFT HIGH THE CROSS

Based on the records released by the Red Cross in June 1958, it is believed that Sister Teresa Benedicta—Edith Stein—died on August 9, 1942. When the train carrying the Jewish Catholics from Holland arrived at Auschwitz, the prisoners were said to be mental patients. Instead of assigning them to work groups, they were all taken immediately from the train to the gas chamber. After being killed by poisonous gas, their bodies were burned to ashes.

As word of this terrible tragedy spread around the world, there was outrage and great sadness. For her religious community, the Discalced Carmelites, Edith Stein was one more beautiful jewel in the crown surrounding Our Lady of Mount Carmel.

People familiar with the life and work of Edith Stein before and after her entrance into the Carmelites petitioned the Church to begin the process leading to sainthood. For other people, however, questions remained. *Was she really a saint? And if she was, how about Rosa and her other companions? Some people insist that Edith Stein died because she was a Jew, like countless others. Was the Church right to canonize her?*

Something very unusual occurred when the Church investigated Edith's holiness. Ordinarily, persons are declared saints because they were martyred *or* because they lived a life of heroic virtue. Edith Stein was found to have lived a life of holiness and *also* to have been a true martyr. Her virtue, especially her charity, grew stronger and deeper every day. This was testified to by the people who knew her. However, it was her willing acceptance of the cross that made her a martyr. In fact, when they were arrested she told Rosa, "Let us go to die with our people."

What can we learn from Saint Edith Stein?

Sometimes we can dream of living in different situations. We can wish that things were better or easier for us. But with God's help, it's possible to find peace and happiness in our own here and now, just as Edith did. There were many difficulties in Edith's life. She faced up to each of them with courage. She was determined to overcome obstacles, beginning with the death of her father.

❖ She grew up in a one-parent home. Her mother worked all day.

❖ At fourteen, Edith stopped practicing her faith. She spent most of her youth searching for truth in philosophy. When she did discover this truth, it turned out to be God, who gave us Jesus Christ and his Church. Her conversion caused much pain to those she loved most. They felt betrayed.

❖ She was told by her spiritual advisor that she should not enter the convent, but find ways to be an apostle in the world. Edith gave herself generously to the life of teacher and lecturer.

❖ Although she was a very qualified doctor of philosophy, she was refused a position as professor because she was Jewish and a woman. Edith continued to try to overcome this prejudice, but always in peace.

❖ Her student days had prepared her for a life in the world of intellectuals. Yet God called her to one of the strictest religious orders in the Church. It seemed to some people that the Carmelite life of enclosure, prayer, penance, and simplicity was a waste of her talent. And then there was her martyrdom.

Sometimes our plans are changed by circumstances we can't control. At other times it may be other choices we make, or decisions forced upon us which cause us sorrow and pain. With Saint Edith, we can try to keep the cross of Jesus always before our eyes and live our lives in God's hands. This is the real secret of the saints.

A Miracle for Teresia Benedicta McCarthy

Every canonization, or the raising of a person to sainthood, requires a miracle. For Edith Stein the miracle took place through a number of coincidences.

In 1987, the McCarthys of Brockton, Massachusetts were a very happy family. Charles and Mary were proud of their twelve beautiful children. The older, college age children had been caring for the younger ones for a whole week while their parents were on a retreat. But when the couple returned home on March 20, they learned that their youngest daughter, two-year-old Teresia Benedicta, had been rushed to the hospital. She had found and opened the bottle of Tylenol that the older children were using to treat the flu. Now she was on a respirator awaiting a liver transplant. Her condition was very critical.

Charles, who is a Catholic priest of the ancient Melkite Rite, had everyone pray to the family's favorite patroness, Edith Stein, for a miraculous cure. To express his complete confidence that God would cure his daughter through Edith Stein's intercession, Father McCarthy kept his promise to preach a retreat in North Dakota. Good news arrived just as he finished.

To the delight of the McCarthy family and the amazement of the doctors, little Benedicta regained her health without ever having the liver transplant. The doctors willingly testified that her cure had to be miraculous. Ten years later, after a very thorough examination of all the facts, the Church declared that the cure of Benedicta McCarthy was truly a miracle worked by God to honor his servant, Edith Stein.

Benedicta McCarthy, who's now a high school student, doesn't remember any of the details of her illness or of her cure. But she believes in her special saint. Saint Edith Stein's hand has been on her family for many years. Her father was ordained a priest on August 9, which is the date of Saint

Edith's martyrdom. Before her birth, Benedicta's parents had decided to name their next daughter for Edith Stein. Imagine how amazed they were when she was born on August 9! It seemed that Edith was showing her willingness to become a part of the McCarthy family, too.

On October 11, 1998, the entire McCarthy family went to Rome to witness the solemn canonization of their special patron by Pope John Paul II.

On October 1, 1999, Pope John Paul II declared Saint Edith Stein to be one of the heavenly co-patronesses of all of Europe, together with Saint Bridget of Sweden and Saint Catherine of Siena.

Prayer

Saint Edith, you're an example to those of us who are students. From the day you asked for "school" as a birthday present to the day you graduated from the university, you were always eager and happy to learn. Help me to appreciate school. Encourage me to never give up when my studies seem difficult. Teach me to enjoy the many wonderful things I learn. They're all gifts from God!

You also show me the importance of being a good friend, Saint Edith. You were always ready to help anyone who was struggling. Help me to be kind and generous with everyone I meet.

But the most important thing I can learn from you is how to love the cross of Jesus. You teach me that the cross is really a sign of God's special love for me. When I have a problem, or something to suffer, remind me that God has a plan for my life and that my suffering has value. I want to follow Jesus as you did—no matter what. Pray for me, Saint Edith. Amen.

Glossary

Aryan—member of the Indo-European language group. Mistakenly used to describe a non-Jewish Caucasian.

Anti-Semitism—opposition to the Semitic peoples, especially the Jews.

Canteen—a military shop where food is served and sold.

Cloister—parts of a convent/monastery reserved to the nuns/monks.

Contemplative life—the life of prayer and meditation, especially in monasteries.

Day of Atonement—an important Jewish holy day; the day to express sorrow for sins and to do penance.

Dissertation—a very detailed and well-prepared discussion of a topic submitted for a university degree.

Dowry—the amount of money given for the support of someone entering religious life.

Frau—"Mrs." in German.

Fraulein—"Miss" in German.

Gestapo—the secret police of Nazi Germany.

Grille—the screen separating cloistered religious from their visitors.

Herr—"Mr." in German.

Mystic—one who seeks knowledge of God by prayer and contemplation.

Novice mistress—the nun who teaches the young women preparing to take vows in the community.

Phenomenology—a method of thinking (philosophy) which attempts to explain what can be seen and experienced.

Philosophy/philosophical—the science of how we think; the nature of things of philosophy.

Prioress—the superior of a house of a women's religious order.

Provincial—the superior of a specific territory in which there are several religious houses of the same community, for example, the Carmelites.

Psychology—the study of the human mind and how it works.

Rabbi—a Jewish religious leader/teacher.

Synagogue—the meeting place for Jewish worship and instruction.

Thesis—the organization of the ideas that one intends to prove or defend.

Vespers—evening prayer.

Daughters of St. Paul

| We Pray | We Preach | We Praise |

Centering our lives on Jesus, Way, Truth, Life

Witnessing to the joy of living totally for Jesus

Sharing Jesus with people through various forms of media: books, music, video, & multimedia

If you would like more information on following Jesus and spreading His Gospel

as a Daughter of St. Paul…

contact:

Vocation Director
Daughters of St. Paul
78 Fort Place
Staten Island, NY 10301
(718) 447-5086
e-mail: vocations@pauline.com
or visit www.pauline.org

Pauline

The Daughters of St. Paul operate book and media centers at the following addresses. Visit, call or write the one nearest you today, or find us on the World Wide Web, www.pauline.org

CALIFORNIA
3908 Sepulveda Blvd., Culver City, CA 90230; 310-397-8676
5945 Balboa Ave., San Diego, CA 92111; 858-565-9181
46 Geary Street, San Francisco, CA 94108; 415-781-5180

FLORIDA
145 S.W. 107th Ave., Miami, FL 33174; 305-559-6715

HAWAII
1143 Bishop Street, Honolulu, HI 96813; 808-521-2731
Neighbor Islands call: 800-259-8463

ILLINOIS
172 N. Michigan Ave., Chicago, IL 60601; 312-346-4228

LOUISIANA
4403 Veterans Blvd., Metairie, LA 70006; 504-887-7631

MASSACHUSETTS
Rte. 1, 885 Providence Hwy., Dedham, MA 02026; 781-326-5385

MISSOURI
9804 Watson Rd., St. Louis, MO 63126; 314-965-3512

NEW JERSEY
561 U.S. Route 1, Wick Plaza, Edison, NJ 08817; 732-572-1200

NEW YORK
150 East 52nd Street, New York, NY 10022; 212-754-1110
78 Fort Place, Staten Island, NY 10301; 718-447-5071

OHIO
2105 Ontario Street (at Prospect Ave.), Cleveland, OH 44115; 216-621-9427

PENNSYLVANIA
9171-A Roosevelt Blvd., Philadelphia, PA 19114; 215-676-9494

SOUTH CAROLINA
243 King Street, Charleston, SC 29401; 843-577-0175

TENNESSEE
4811 Poplar Ave., Memphis, TN 38117 901-761-2987

TEXAS
114 Main Plaza, San Antonio, TX 78205; 210-224-8101

VIRGINIA
1025 King Street, Alexandria, VA 22314; 703-549-3806

CANADA
3022 Dufferin Street, Toronto, Ontario, Canada M6B 3T5; 416-781-9131
1155 Yonge Street, Toronto, Ontario, Canada M4T 1W2; 416-934-3440

¡También somos su fuente para libros, videos y música en español!